Two Mites

Stephenie Bunte
and Hayley Keenon

WESTBOW
PRESS®
A DIVISION OF THOMAS NELSON
& ZONDERVAN

Scripture taken from the Holy Bible, NEW INTERNATIONAL VERSION®. Copyright © 1973, 1978, 1984 by Biblica, Inc. All rights reserved worldwide. Used by permission. NEW INTERNATIONAL VERSION® and NIV® are registered trademarks of Biblica, Inc. Use of either trademark for the offering of goods or services requires the prior written consent of Biblica US, Inc.

Scripture taken from the New King James Version. Copyright © 1979, 1980, 1982 by Thomas Nelson, Inc. Used by permission. All rights reserved.

Scripture quotations are from The Holy Bible, English Standard Version® (ESV®), copyright © 2001 by Crossway, a publishing ministry of Good News Publishers. Used by permission. All rights reserved.

NET Bible® copyright ©1996-2006 by Biblical Studies Press, L.L.C. http://netbible.com All rights reserved.

Scripture quotations taken from the Holy Bible, New Living Translation, Copyright © 1996, 2004. Used by permission of Tyndale House Publishers, Inc., Wheaton, Illinois 60189. All rights reserved.

WestBow Press books may be ordered through booksellers or by contacting:

WestBow Press
A Division of Thomas Nelson & Zondervan
1663 Liberty Drive
Bloomington, IN 47403
www.westbowpress.com
1 (866) 928-1240

ISBN: 978-1-5127-3255-9 (sc)

Library of Congress Control Number: 2016903191

Print information available on the last page.

WestBow Press rev. date: 03/02/2016

Dedicated to Bro. Mike
Who always encouraged us and believed in us,
even when we didn't believe in ourselves.

Also, special thanks to
Our families,
Our church
Rachelle,
Bro. Donnie,
Billy & Kat
Your never-ending prayers and support
meant more than you will ever know.

Contents

Tips

- Feel free to add things, take out things, use different verses, whatever. Make it your own! This is not a curriculum you have to follow word by word.

- Speak very slowly. Don't rush it.

- Change your voice. Make it go up and down. Exaggerate.

- Don't be afraid to be silly. Have fun! The sillier you are the more you get the kid's attention.

- Teachers can ask the questions, but if you know kid's names the puppets could call them out and ask the questions. It surprises and excites the kids that the puppet knows their name and it helps keep all the kids from yelling out answers at the same time.

God's Creation

Genesis 1:1–2:3

Memory Verses

All things were created by him. John 1:3

He has made everything beautiful in its time. Ecclesiastes 3:11

Taylor: Hey!

Jordan: Hey!

Taylor: Remember the other day when we were sitting outside?

Jordan: Yeah. Why?

Taylor: Well, I was just thinking how pretty everything was. The trees, the grass…

Jordan: The flowers.

Taylor: The sky.

Jordan: The birds.

Taylor: Yeah. It's all so amazing.

Jordan: You know what's even more amazing?

Taylor: What?

Jordan: The One who created all those things.

Taylor: What do you mean?

Jordan: You know about the story of God's creation. (to kids) Did you know that God made everything? It took him six days to do it. Before He created anything, it was dark. So on the first day He started out by making light.

Taylor: Then, on the second day, He made the pretty blue sky, the white puffy clouds, and the big beautiful ocean.

Jordan: I went to the ocean. I made a sand castle and looked for seashells. It was so cool! What did God make on the third day?

Taylor: He created land. He made the grass, the trees, the pretty flowers, and the big tall mountains.

Jordan: On the fourth day, He made the bright, warm sunshine, the moon, and the shiny stars.

Taylor: The next day, He created all the birds and the sea creatures.

Jordan: Like camels!

Taylor: Camels? Camels don't live in the ocean.

Jordan: Oh. Well, what lives in the ocean?

Taylor: Fish, whales, sharks, sea turtles and octopuses live in the ocean. Do you know what God made on the sixth day?

Jordan: On the sixth day, God created all the land animals. Like horses, sheep, and… hmmm. (to kids) Help me out here, kids. What are some other animals that God made?

Taylor and Jordan: (as kids name animals) Yeah. That's right. Good job. That's a good one. (Etc.)

Taylor: Then God made something special. He made a man. His name was Adam. And God let Adam name all the animals.

Jordan: He got to name all of them?

Taylor: Every one of them. God was very happy with everything He had made. So on the seventh day, He rested.

Jordan: Wow. Isn't God amazing?

Taylor: He sure is. He made all of us and He loves us very much. Let's thank Him right now for everything He made.

Jordan: Okay. Everybody, bow your heads.

Taylor: Thank you God, for making this beautiful place for us to live. Thank you for the warm sunshine, and the pretty flowers.

Jordan: Thank you for the beautiful ocean, all the animals, and thank you for loving each and every one of us. Amen.

Taylor: Thanks for joining us today!

Jordan: We will see you all later.

Taylor and Jordan: Bye!

Questions:

What did God create? (Everything.)

How many days did it take Him? (Six days.)

Was He happy with everything He made? (Yes)

Adam and Eve

Genesis 2:4 - 3:24

Taylor: Hey guys! Where's Jordan?

Jordan: Hi, everyone!

Taylor: There you are. We were looking for you.

Jordan: What's going on?

Taylor: Well, I was going to tell our friends about Adam and Eve, and I thought you might want to help me tell the story.

Jordan: Sure! You start it.

Taylor: Well, you know how in the beginning God created the world and everything in it?

Jordan: Yeah.

Taylor: Well, He wanted someone to enjoy it all.

Jordan: Of course!

Taylor: So He created a man named Adam.

Jordan: Yeah, I know about him. He's the one that helped God name all the animals, like the strong lions and tall giraffes.

Taylor: Yes, He did. And the long sneaky snakes! Ssss!

Jordan: Yes. And… the big scarrrry bears!

Taylor: Well, Adam was the first man on earth, and even though there were lots of cool animals to play with, Adam was lonely.

Jordan: Well, I'm sure he wanted someone he could talk to.

Taylor: He did. So God made a woman named Eve and she became Adam's wife.

Jordan: But she sure got Adam into trouble. See, there was a mean, sneaky snake. And he told Eve…

Taylor: Hey! I have an idea. Let's act out the story.

Jordan: Ok! I'll be Eve and you be the snake.

Taylor: Ok!

Jordan: (In high pitched voice) Hi. I'm Eve. I sure am hungry.

Taylor: Why don't you eat some of the fruit from this tree?

Jordan: Oh, God said to never eat the fruit from THAT tree or I will die!

Taylor: You won't die. You will be just like God. Go ahead. It's very tasty.

Jordan: Well, maybe just a bite. Ooh, that's good! I'm going to take some to Adam. (in normal voice) Ok now you be Adam.

Taylor: Ok. (In deep voice) Hi. I'm Adam.

Jordan: (in high pitched voice) Adam?

Taylor: Yes, Eve?

Jordan: Try this fruit. It's very good.

Taylor: Mm mm. That's good. Where did you get it?

Jordan: Well, I got it from the tree God told us not to eat off of.

Taylor: Oh. It sure is… AAAAGGGGHHHHHH!!!!

Jordan: No, it's ok! The snake told me we wouldn't die. We will be just like God!

Taylor: Oh no, this isn't good. We better go hide!

Jordan: Okay, let's go!

Taylor: (Normal voice) Man that snake sure was mean and tricky, huh?

Jordan: He sure was. God was very sad that Adam and Eve disobeyed Him. He told them they couldn't live in His beautiful garden anymore.

Taylor: But you know what?

Jordan: What?

Taylor: Even though they disobeyed God, He still loved them.

Jordan: Isn't it nice to know that we have a God that loves us so much?

Taylor: It sure is. And He will always love us. And we should do our best to always obey His commands.

Jordan: Yep! Because He knows what's best for us.

Taylor: That's right. Man. All this story telling makes me hungry!

Jordan: Yeah, me, too. Let's go eat.

Taylor: We will see you next time!.

Taylor and Jordan: Bye!

Questions:

Was Adam lonely? (Yes.)

Who was the friend God gave Adam? (Eve.)

Who told Eve to disobey God? (The snake.)

Did God still love them? (Yes.)

Noah's Ark

Genesis 6:13–9:17

Jordan: (Hiding under blanket, whimpering.)

Taylor: What's wrong with you?

Jordan: It's storming outside and I'm scared. Aaah! Did you hear that?

Taylor: Hear what?

Jordan: That thunder! Aaah! Did you see that lightning?

Taylor: Why are you so scared? I mean if it didn't storm the trees, the flowers, and our gardens wouldn't grow. And just think about that beautiful rainbow that God leaves after it rains.

Jordan: But what if it floods? I CAN'T SWIM! (Starts crying.)

Taylor: It's not going to flood. Don't you know the story about the rainbow?

Jordan: The story about the rainbow? No.

Taylor: Well, it all started with… (Jordan coughs.) Anyways, it all started with… (Jordan coughs again.) I'm trying to tell a story!

Jordan: Sorry.

Taylor: It all started with…

Jordan: Ah… ah… ACHOO!

Taylor: Are you okay now?

Jordan: Yes.

Taylor: It all started with a guy named Noah. God told him to build a big, huge boat for him, his family, and two of every kind of animal there is. Like lions, and tigers, and bears!

Jordan: Oh my! That would have to be one big boat!

Taylor: Yep! But people thought Noah was crazy and they called him mean names and laughed at him.

Jordan: Well, that's not very nice.

Taylor: No, it's not. But he did what God told him to anyway, and he built the boat. He loaded his family and two of every kind of animal on the boat. Then it rained for forty days and forty nights!

Jordan: Forty days and forty nights?

Taylor: Yes. And the water flooded the whole earth. It even covered the mountains!

Jordan: I bet that was scary.

Taylor: Maybe. But Noah trusted God. The water finally went down and they landed softly on a mountain. God made the rainbow as a promise that He would never flood the earth again.

Jordan: Never?

Taylor: Never ever. So see? No worries. It may rain and storm, but it will never flood the earth again. So how do you feel about storms now?

Jordan: Well, I guess I feel a little better now. And the flowers do need water.

Taylor: Good. Well. See ya later!

Jordan: Wait! Don't go!

Taylor: You're not still scared are you?

Jordan: What? No. Aaah! Thunder! (Hides under blanket.)

Taylor: (Laughs.) Oh my.

Questions:
How many of each animal went on the boat? (Two)
How long did it rain? (Forty days and forty nights.)
What did God put in the sky as a promise? (A rainbow.)

Joseph

Genesis 37:1-41:57

Taylor: Hey!

Jordan: Hey. Is that a new coat?

Taylor: Yeah. Isn't it pretty?

Jordan: It's very pretty.

Taylor: Thank you. My daddy got it for me.

Jordan: Well that was nice of him. It reminds me of that guy in the Bible with the coat of many colors. What was his name? Moseph? Poseph? No. Zoseph. It was Zoseph.

Taylor: I think you mean Joseph.

Jordan: Joseph! Yeah. I knew that. His daddy gave him a coat with all the colors of the rainbow in it.

Taylor: Yeah, but I'm glad I don't have eleven angry brothers like Joseph did.

Jordan: Joseph had eleven brothers?!

Taylor: Yep.

Jordan: Wow. That's a lot of brothers. Why were they angry?

Taylor: Because their daddy didn't make any coats for them. Only for Joseph. Man, they sure were jealous.

Jordan: What does jealous mean?

Taylor: It means they wanted what he had. So much that they wanted to kill Joseph!

Jordan: (Gasp.) But they didn't, did they?

Taylor: Nope. Instead they sent him to a faraway place called Egypt. Then they told their dad that Joseph was killed by a wild animal.

Jordan: They lied?

Taylor: They sure did.

Jordan: I bet their daddy was sad. And I bet Joseph was sad. And scared!

Taylor: Well, he was. But he trusted God and God took care of him.

Jordan: How?

Taylor: God gave Joseph a special gift.

Jordan: Ooh what was it?

Taylor: Joseph was able to understand dreams.

Jordan: Wait, what?

Taylor: One night Pharaoh, the king of Egypt, had a dream. But he didn't know what it meant. So he asked Joseph.

Jordan: And Joseph understood it?

Taylor: Yep. God was telling Pharaoh about... dun, dun, dun! The future!

Jordan: Oh, what about the future?

Taylor: There would be seven years of good things and seven years of bad things.

Jordan: What did Joseph do?

Taylor: He worked hard so when the bad came he was ready and everyone was taken care of.

Jordan: That was a good idea.

Taylor: It sure was.

Jordan: Wow. Even when things were bad he didn't get mad at God. He trusted God.

Taylor: And God sure took care of him, didn't He?

Jordan: He sure did. I had a dream last night.

Taylor: What was it about?

Jordan: There were hundreds of ice creams trucks, and I had some of every kind of ice cream there was! It was so yummy! What do you think that means?

Taylor: I think that means you've been thinking about the ice cream truck too much. (Laughs.) Come on. Let's go get some ice cream together.

Questions:
Were Joseph's brothers jealous? (Yes.)
Did Joseph get mad at God? (No.)
Did Joseph trust God? (Yes.)
And we need to trust God, too, don't we? (Yes.)

David and Goliath

1 Samuel 17:16-50

Jordan: Hey. How was your day?

Taylor: Good. How was yours?

Jordan: Not very good. I got picked on all day at school.

Taylor: Why?

Jordan: Because I'm little. They laughed at me because I couldn't reach the crayon box on the shelf. And then they said I couldn't play soccer with them because I wasn't big enough. I couldn't do anything. All because I'm so little.

Taylor: Awww. I'm sorry. That's not very nice. Size doesn't matter. David didn't let his size stop him when he fought Goliath. Do you remember that story?

Jordan: Yeah. But I don't mind hearing it again.

Taylor: Well, a long time ago there was a boy named David. His brothers were in the king's army. And the king's army was about to go into battle!

Jordan: Uh, oh.

Taylor: David went to take his brothers some food before this big fight started.

Jordan: Well that was nice of him.

Taylor: It sure was. But when David got there, there was a huge giant named Goliath. And he wanted to fight! But everyone was too scared to fight him. Except David. David was so brave he said he would fight him.

Jordan: He wasn't scared?

Taylor: No. David knew God would help him. Even though all he had was a slingshot.

Jordan: Wow. David really trusted God! What happened then?

Taylor: Well Goliath laughed when he saw David because David was just a little kid. But David slung a rock at Goliath and hit him on the head and killed him!

Jordan: So even though David was little and people made fun of him, he had faith in God, and God helped him.

Taylor: That's right. So do you feel better now?

Jordan: Yeah.

Taylor: Hey. I'm playing soccer with some of my friends this afternoon. Why don't you come and play with us?

Jordan: Okay! Yeah!

Taylor: Cool! Let's go!

Questions:

What was the Giant's name? (Goliath.)

What did David kill Goliath with? (A rock.)

Who helped him? (God.)

Shadrach, Meshach, and Abed-Nego

Daniel 3:1-30

Memory Verses

Never stop praying.
1 Thessalonians 5:17

Don't worry about anything; instead, pray about everything.
Philippians 4:6

Taylor: Hey!

Jordan: Oh my goodness! You know what happened to me the other day?

Taylor: No. What?

Jordan: I was camping with my family and we made a campfire and we were making s'mores.

Taylor: Ooh, I love s'mores!

Jordan: But my s'more caught on fire!

Taylor: Oh no!

Jordan: I got scared so I threw it and it landed in the tent! And the tent caught on fire! But my daddy got the fire out.

Taylor: Were you scared?

Jordan: Yeah. It was really scary. And hot! I'm so glad God protected us.

Taylor: Yeah, me too. That reminds me of a story in the Bible about three men who were thrown into the fire, and God protected them, too.

Jordan: Oh! You mean Medrach, Abedrach, and Shabed-Nego!

Taylor: I think you mean Shadrach, Meshach, and Abed-Nego.

Jordan: Yeah, that's what I said.

Taylor: No, you said… never mind. Hey, let's tell them the story. (speaking slowly, in a deep voice.) Once upon a time in a far away city called Babylon, there lived three men named Shadrach. Meshach. (pause for effect) And Abed-Nego.

Jordan: What are you doing?

Taylor: I'm telling the story.

Jordan: Well, we don't have to tell it like that.

Taylor: I was trying to make it scary.

Jordan: It's not a scary story!

Taylor: Oh. Okay. Well, there were three boys named Shadrach, Meshach, and Abed-Nego. They worked for King Nebuchadnezzar.

Jordan: Nebuchadnezzar? Wow. That's hard to say.

Taylor: Can you say that? Try it with us. King Nebuchadnezzar.

Jordan: Good job!

Taylor: One day King Nebuchadnezzar decided he wanted everyone to pray to his statue.

Jordan: What? You're only supposed to pray to God.

Taylor: That's right. And he told everyone if they didn't pray to his statue, he would throw them into a fire!

Jordan: Oh, no!

Taylor: But Shadrach, Meshach, and Abed-Nego still prayed to God. They weren't scared.

Jordan: They weren't?

Taylor: Nope. They trusted God. And when the king threw them into the fire, they didn't even get burned!

Jordan: Wow! You mean God saved them?

Taylor: That's right. Because they loved God and only prayed to Him, He protected them.

Jordan: Just like he protected me when we went camping.

Taylor: God protects us, too. He loves us. We need to trust Him and pray every day.

Jordan: I know I will. Hey, we are going camping again this weekend. You wanna go with us? I promise I won't set your tent on fire!

Taylor: (laughs) Okay. I better go pack! See you later!

Jordan: Bye!

Questions:
Did Shadrach, Meshach, and Abed-Nego pray to the statue? (No.)
Who threw them into the fire? (King Nebuchadnezzar.)
Did they get burned? (No.)
God protected them didn't He? (Yes.)

Daniel and the Lion's Den

Daniel 6:1-28

Taylor: Hello! Guess what? It's story time!

Jordan: That's right!

Taylor: And today we are talking about Daniel and the Lion's Den.

Jordan: Oooh! That sounds like a good story!

Taylor: It is. A long, long time ago there was a man named Daniel. And Daniel's best friend was King Darius.

Jordan: Wow! I bet it was cool being best friends with a king!

Taylor: Well, it was, but some of the other guys got real jealous of Daniel being the king's best friend.

Jordan: Uh oh.

Taylor: So they started watching Daniel to see if he did anything wrong. That way they could tell the king and Daniel would get in trouble.

Jordan: That's not very nice.

Taylor: No, it's not. But guess what? Daniel didn't do anything wrong. All he did was pray by his window every day.

Jordan: So what did they do?

Taylor: Well, these guys were pretty mean. So they told the king he should make a new rule.

Jordan: What kind of rule?

Taylor: For thirty days nobody could pray to anyone except King Darius.

Jordan: What? That's crazy! You're only supposed to pray to God.

Taylor: That's right. But the king made the rule anyway.

Jordan: What if people didn't want to pray to the king?

Taylor: Then they would be thrown into the lion's den. RAWR!

Jordan: Agh!

Taylor: But that didn't stop Daniel.

Jordan: It didn't?

Taylor: Nope. Daniel loved God so much, he kept on praying to him every day. So when those mean men saw him praying, they took Daniel to the king.

Jordan: What happened?

Taylor: The king didn't want to punish his best friend Daniel. But a rule is a rule. So Daniel was thrown into the lion's den.

Jordan: (Gasp!) With all those hungry lions?

Taylor: Yep. But he didn't get eaten.

Jordan: What? How?

Taylor: Daniel prayed all night to God. And God sent an angel to shut the lion's mouths so they couldn't eat him.

Jordan: Wow!

Taylor: The next morning King Darius ran to the lion's den. When he saw that Daniel was still alive, He praised God for protecting Daniel. And he never made a silly rule like that again.

Jordan: You see Daniel knew if he kept praying to God he might die. But he also knew that praying to God is very important. God protected him for doing what was right. We need to do what's right, too.

Taylor: Yep. Cause if you don't, I'll throw you in a lion's den!

Jordan: Aaaah!

Taylor: I'm just kidding.

Jordan: (laughs) Man. (yawns) I'm sleepy.

Taylor: (yawns) Me, too. It's my nap time.

Jordan: Mine too. (yawns) Good night.

Taylor: Good night.

Taylor and Jordan: (go down and start snoring.)

Questions:

Did Daniel get thrown into a den of elephants? (No.)

Did Daniel get thrown into a den of lions? (Yes.)

Did Daniel pray to God or the king? (God.)

Did he get eaten? (No.)

God protected Daniel, didn't He? (Yes.)

Jonah and the Whale

Jonah 1:1–3:10

Taylor: Hi Jordan. Guess what!

Jordan: What?

Taylor: I went to the pet store the other day!

Jordan: You did?

Taylor: Uh huh! I saw puppies, kittens, and fish. There was one fish that was HUGE!

Jordan: Really? I bet it wasn't as big as the one that swallowed Jonah.

Taylor: No probably not. (to audience) Hey, have you heard about Jonah and the whale? Let's tell them the story.

Jordan: Okay. (Pause) I thought you were going to tell them the story!

Taylor: Well I thought you were going to tell them!

Jordan: Okay. I'll start and you jump in.

Taylor: Okay.

Jordan: Once upon a time there was a man named Jonah. And God told Jonah to go to the city of Nineveh.

Taylor: Hee hee. Nineveh. That's a funny name for a city. Nineveh. Nineveh!

Jordan: Excuse me. I'm telling a story here.

Taylor: Sorry.

Jordan: Anyways, God told Jonah to go to the city of Nineveh. But Jonah didn't want to go to Nineveh. You know why?

Taylor: No. Why?

Jordan: Because the people there were mean! So Jonah got on a boat and tried to run away from God.

Taylor: But you can't hide from God. God sees everything.

Jordan: That's right. So God sent a giant whale and it swallowed Jonah! It was dark inside the whale's belly, and Jonah didn't have a flashlight.

Taylor: I bet it was cold and wet, too.

Jordan: And Jonah didn't have a blanket either!

Taylor: And it was probably stinky, too. Pee-yew!

Jordan: Yeah, and he probably had seaweed tangled in his hair.

Taylor: Ew. Jonah was inside the whale for three whole days! Jonah prayed to God and God made the whale spit Jonah out! God told Jonah again to go to Nineveh.

Jordan: So Jonah went to Nineveh and told the people they needed to start being nice. If they didn't they would be in big trouble. The people of Nineveh were sorry for being so mean. So God forgave them.

Taylor: Yep. God always forgives us if we are sorry.

Jordan: That's right. God wants us to be nice and love each other.

Taylor: Hey, I know a way I can be nice.

Jordan: How?

Taylor: Would you like to go with me to the pet store? I'll show you that big fish!

Jordan: Yeah!

Taylor: Okay! Let's go!

Questions:

What swallowed Jonah? (A whale.)

How long was Jonah in the whale's belly? (Three days.)

Did God forgive the people of Nineveh? (Yes.)

Jesus Walks on Water

Matthew 14:22-31

Memory Verses

Whenever I am afraid, I will trust in You. Psalm 56:3

Trust in the Lord with all your heart, and lean not on your own understanding. Proverbs 3:5

Jordan: Hey guys! (looks around for Taylor) Hang on, let me find Taylor. (goes backstage)

Taylor: Ugh. Almost. Ugh, no!

Jordan: Taylor, what are you doing?

Taylor: I'm trying to walk on this water.

Jordan: What? You know that only Jesus can do that.

Taylor: Well, I was at least going to try.

Jordan: Will you stop being so silly? It's story time. (both come out.) We should tell our friends about when Jesus walked on water.

Taylor: Okay, yeah. You go ahead and I'll jump in.

Jordan: Okay. This story takes place a long time ago, by the sea.

Taylor: Oooh, I like the sea!

Jordan: Jesus and His disciples were about to cross the sea. The disciples got into the boat, but Jesus decided not to.

Taylor: Why? He can't cross the sea if he doesn't get in the boat.

Jordan: Jesus decided to go up the mountain and pray.

Taylor: Why did He want to go up the mountain to pray?

Jordan: Because He wanted to be by Himself.

Taylor: Oh. What did the disciples do?

Jordan: They set sail without Him. But while they were sailing, a big storm came! The waves rocked the boat back and forth, (both puppets move side to side) and back and forth, and back and forth…

Taylor: Stop! I'm getting seasick!

Jordan: Sorry. Anyways, the disciples were scared. They didn't know what to do. Then they saw something. Someone was walking on the water!

Taylor: (Gasp) Was it Jesus?

Jordan: Yep. But when the disciples saw Him they were scared.

Taylor: Why?

18

Jordan: They thought He was a ghost! But Jesus told them not to be afraid. So Peter asked if he could walk on the water, too. Jesus said yes. So Peter stood up, got out of the boat and started walking on the water!

Taylor: How could Peter walk on the water?

Jordan: He had faith in God. But then he saw some huge waves coming right at him! He got scared and forgot to trust God. So he began to fall in the water.

Taylor: Oh no!

Jordan: But Jesus reached out and grabbed him before he fell in the water. See? Jesus is always there for us. Even when we don't trust Him.

Taylor: That's right. Jesus loves us. He wants to take care of us. We just have to trust Him.

Jordan: Yep. The Bible says, "Trust in the Lord with all your heart."

Taylor: That's right. Man, all this talk about water made me thirsty. Let's go get something to drink.

Jordan: Ok. Come on.

Questions:
Did Jesus walk on the water? (Yes.)
Who else walked on the water? (Peter.)
But he got scared, didn't he? (Yes.)
We need to trust God when we are scared, don't we? (Yes.)

Zacchaeus

Luke 19:1-10

Jordan: Hi, Taylor.

Taylor: Hi, Jordan.

Jordan: How tall are you?

Taylor: I'm three feet and seven inches tall. Why?

Jordan: Aw man! You're taller than me, too!

Taylor: What?

Jordan: Everyone is taller than I am. I feel like Zacchaeus.

Taylor: Who?

Jordan: Zacchaeus.

Taylor: Oh yeah. People didn't like Zacchaeus though.

Jordan: Why?

Taylor: Because he stole people's money.

Jordan: He did?

Taylor: Yep. And he used it to buy himself stuff. He had fancy clothes, and a nice big house. But you know what he didn't have?

Jordan: What?

Taylor: He didn't have any friends.

Jordan: I bet he was lonely.

Taylor: He was. But one day Jesus came to town. Zacchaeus wanted to meet Him. But Zacchaeus was so short, he couldn't see where Jesus was.

Jordan: What did he do?

Taylor: Well, he climbed way up in a tree.

Jordan: Did he see a bird's nest? Baby birds are so cute!

Taylor: No. But he saw Jesus! And Jesus saw him. Jesus walked right up and said, "Zacchaeus, you come down. I'm going to your house today."

Jordan: Wow! That would be so cool if Jesus came to your house!

Taylor: Zacchaeus thought so, too. He was so happy. Jesus wanted to be his friend.

Jordan: Now he wasn't lonely anymore.

Taylor: Nope. In fact, he was so happy he gave all the people their money back. He even gave them more than he took!

Jordan: Well, that sure was nice of him.

Taylor: Yes, it was. Jesus loved Zacchaeus and wanted to be his friend. But He also wanted Zacchaeus to do the right thing.

Jordan: That's right. God loves us even when we do bad things. And if we say we are sorry He will forgive us.

Taylor: But it makes God so much happier when we do the right thing.

Jordan: Well, I sure like for God to be happy with me. Aren't you glad we have a God who loves us so much?

Taylor: I sure am. It doesn't matter if we are tall or short, big or small, God loves us all.

Jordan: I guess it's not so bad being short. Let's go play!

Taylor: Okay!

Jordan: Bye, everyone!

Taylor: See you next time.

Questions:

Was Zacchaeus short? (Yes.)

What did he climb so he could see? (A tree.)

Who did he see when he looked down? (Jesus.)

Two Fish and Five Loaves

John 6:1 – 13

Memory Verses

And God will generously provide all you need.
2 Corinthians 9:8

Taylor: Hey guys!

Jordan: Hey!

Taylor: Are we going to tell a story today?

Jordan: Yes we are.

Taylor: Can we tell them that story in the Bible where God provided all that food for over five thousand people?

Jordan: Oh yes, I love that story! Taylor, would you like to start it?

Taylor: Okay. It all started one day when Jesus was riding in His boat, and over five thousand people followed Him.

Jordan: Wow! That's a lot of people! Why did they follow Him?

Taylor: Because they had heard about all the things Jesus had done.

Jordan: Like what?

Taylor: Well, He made sick people feel better. No matter what was wrong. If they had a tummy ache, or a sore throat, or a scratch, He made it go away.

Jordan: Even a broken arm?

Taylor: That's right. He could make anything better.

Jordan: Wow!

Taylor: So all these people came to see Jesus. That would be so cool to see Jesus!

Jordan: It sure would! He talked to them all day. After being there so long they got hungry. But they didn't have any food. Until a little boy brought them a basket with two fish and five loaves of bread.

Taylor: That was really sweet of him.

Jordan: It sure was. That was all the food he had and he gave it to others.

Taylor: What kind of fish did he have?

Jordan: I don't know.

Taylor: Was it goldfish?

Jordan: What? No! You don't eat goldfish!

Taylor: Was it catfish? I love me some catfish!

Jordan: I don't know. It was just fish.

Taylor: Ok.

Jordan: Jesus prayed and started passing out the food. He fed all the people until they were stuffed! They even had food left over!

Taylor: Wow! They only had two fish and five loaves of bread, but God still fed over five thousand people! Isn't God amazing?

Jordan: He sure is. God loves us and always takes care of us.

Taylor: Yep. Hey, Jordan?

Jordan: What?

Taylor: Can we go get some catfish? I'm hungry.

Jordan: (Laughs.) Sure, let's go.

Taylor: We will see you guys later!

Taylor and Jordan: Bye!

Questions:

How many fish did they have? (Two.)

How many loaves of bread did they have? (Five.)

How many people were there? (Five thousand.)

Did God provide enough for all five thousand people? (Yes.)

Thanksgiving

Taylor: Hey guys! Does anyone know what's coming up? Thanksgiving! I'm gonna have turkey, and dressing, and mashed potatoes, and pumpkin pie!

Jordan: (comes up) Ugh! I'm so mad!

Taylor: Why? What's wrong?

Jordan: I had a bad day. I got hit at school. I fell off the slide and hurt my knee, and when I went to swing, it was broken.

Taylor: Man, you had a rough day! At least you have band aids.

Jordan: And that's supposed to make me feel better? Why are you so happy all the time?

Taylor: Because I'm thankful for what I have. Just think. Some kids don't have band aids when they get hurt.

Jordan: Really? I didn't know that.

Taylor: Yeah. So you should be thankful that you do. You can even get cool ones with cartoons on them! God has given us so much.

Jordan: Well, maybe He has given you a lot. All I have is a bruise on my arm, a sore knee, and a broken swing.

Taylor: Are you forgetting how Jesus died on the cross for our sins? He didn't have to do that. But He loved us so much. I'm most thankful for Jesus.

Jordan: Well, I'm thankful for that. But I don't know what else I have to be thankful for.

Taylor: There has got to be something. What about your family? Or the house you live in? The food you have to eat? Or your teddy bear that keeps you safe and comfy while you're sleeping? And what about your new puppy you got for your birthday?

Jordan: I guess you're right. I do have a lot to be thankful for, huh? Let's say a thank you prayer to God right now.

Taylor: Sure!

Jordan: Thank you Lord for helping us feel better when we have a bad day.

Taylor: Thank you for taking care of us and keeping us safe.

Jordan: Thank you for giving us a family to celebrate Thanksgiving with.

Taylor: And thank you Lord for dying on the cross so we can go to Heaven.

Taylor and Jordan: Amen.

Jordan: Hey you know what else I'm thankful for?

Taylor: What?

Jordan: Games! Like hide and go seek! Try to find me. Ready, set, go! (goes down)

Taylor: Hey! Wait! I wasn't ready! (goes down)

Jordan: (backstage) You'll never find me!

Taylor: (backstage) Oh yes I will!

Questions:

Who did Jesus die on the cross for? (Me, us, everyone)

Are you thankful for Jesus?

Christmas

Taylor: Hey guys!

Jordan: Guess what! Guess what! Guess what!

Taylor: What? What is it?

Jordan: Christmas is coming!

Taylor: I know! I'm so excited! Hey since Christmas is coming let's tell the Christmas story today.

Jordan: Okay! You know I have a friend who doesn't know the Christmas story. She thinks Christmas is just about Santa Claus bringing her gifts.

Taylor: What? No. That's not what Christmas is about. It's about celebrating Jesus' birthday. It all started with a woman named Mary. She was going to have a baby.

Jordan: Mary and her husband Joseph were going to Bethlehem. But they didn't have cars back then.

Taylor: You know what else they didn't have? Ice cream.

Jordan: What does that have to do with the story?

Taylor: I don't know. I just feel like ice cream.

Jordan: Anyways. They didn't have cars. So they had to ride on a donkey!

Taylor: Ooh! I want to ride on a donkey. Hee haw! Hee haw!

Jordan: I know! That would be cool! But they had to ride a long time on that donkey. They were tired. But they couldn't find anywhere to stay. So they had to stay in a barn.

Taylor: With all the animals?

Jordan: Yep. There were probably cows, horses, donkeys, or fluffy white sheep.

Taylor: I bet it was stinky in there with all those animals.

Jordan: Probably. And while they were there Mary had the baby. She wrapped Him up nice and warm and laid him in a manger. He didn't even cry.

Taylor: He didn't?

Jordan: On the same night there were some shepherds watching their sheep. And suddenly an angel appeared before them. They were afraid.

Taylor: I bet. Imagine standing in a field at night time and all of a sudden poof! There's an angel! Aaaah!

Jordan: But he had good news. He told them about baby Jesus being born. So they hurried off to see Him.

Taylor: So that's how Jesus came to earth. And that's what Christmas is about. Celebrating Jesus' birthday and being thankful that He came to save us from our sins.

Jordan: That's right. I am so thankful Jesus came to save us so we could go to Heaven.

Taylor: Me, too. I'm also thankful for ice cream.

Jordan: I think I hear the ice cream truck now.

Taylor: Huh? Where? Ice cream! (goes off stage yelling) Ice cream! Ice cream! Ice cream!

Jordan: Hey! Wait for me! (to kids) Bye! See you next time! Merry Christmas! (leaves yelling) Jordan! Wait for me!

Questions:
Who was born on Christmas Day? (Jesus.)
Did Mary and Joseph have to stay in a barn? (Yes.)
Are you thankful Jesus came to the earth? (Yes.)

Easter

Jordan: Hey. What are you doing?

Taylor: I'm making eggs.

Jordan: Oh, I like mine scrambled.

Taylor: No, no, no. I'm making Easter eggs.

Jordan: Oh. Well, I'd still like mine to be scrambled.

Taylor: You don't scramble Easter eggs, silly.

Jordan: Then what do you do with them?

Taylor: You paint them. Haven't you ever heard of Easter before?

Jordan: Oh, is that where that guy with the big belly, dressed in a red suit comes and puts eggs under your pillow, and takes your tooth?

Taylor: What? No! You're silly! Easter is when we celebrate the day that Jesus rose from the dead.

Jordan: You can't do that. Can you?

Taylor: Jesus did. When Jesus died on the cross for our sins…

Jordan: What's sin?

Taylor: When we do something bad, that's called sin. And we all do bad things sometimes. So we all have sinned.

Jordan: I know I have sinned.

Taylor: But Jesus died on the cross for our sins so that we could go to heaven. We just have to believe in Jesus and ask him to forgive us for our sins.

Jordan: That's it?

Taylor: That's it.

Jordan: But how did He rise from the dead?

Taylor: After he died on the cross they put Him in a tomb and put a big rock in front of it. Then…

Jordan: What's a tomb?

Taylor: It's kind of like a cave.

Jordan: Oh ok, now I get it. My mom has told me about this before.

Taylor: So three days later Mary went to the tomb and the stone was gone! An angel was there and he told her that Jesus was alive. So that's why we celebrate Easter. It's the day that Jesus rose from the dead. Now do you understand?

Jordan: Yes, I understand now. Easter sounds interesting.

Taylor: Hey, do you want to help me make Easter eggs?

Jordan: Sure! I'd still like mine scrambled.

Taylor: Oh no, not this again.

Questions:

What is it called when we do something bad? (Sin)

Who died for our sins? (Jesus)

Why do we celebrate Easter? (Because Jesus rose from the dead)

Mother's Day

Taylor: Hey!

Jordan: Hey!

Taylor: Do you know what Sunday is?

Jordan: No, what?

Taylor: It's Mother's Day!

Jordan: What's Mother's Day?

Taylor: It's a day that we celebrate moms and all that they do for us.

Jordan: Like what?

Taylor: Just think about it. They do everything! They take care of us, tuck us in at night, read us bed time stories, stay up with us all night when we're sick.

Jordan: Yeah. And they take us to soccer practice, feed us, give us hugs when we're sad, give us band aids when we get hurt.

Taylor: That's right. They do all that. But sometimes we forget to tell our moms that we love them. So on Mother's Day we show our mommies just how much we love them!

Jordan: Well I sure love my mommy. How can I show her how much I love her?

Taylor: You can give her great big hugs, and flowers, and presents, make her a card, and tell her how thankful you are that she's your mom.

Jordan: Yeah, last year my daddy and I made breakfast for my mommy and then we went to the park and played together.

Taylor: You can always have fun with your mommy. And we have to remember that even when they tell us "No." Because we're too little to be in charge.

Jordan: Yeah, they know what's best for us! And even when we start throwing a fit and screaming because we didn't get our way, they still love us!

Taylor: The Bible says in Matthew 19:19 it says "Honor your father and mother, and love your neighbor as yourself."

Jordan: I really like that verse.

Taylor: Me, too. It means we have to listen to them no matter what.

Jordan: Hey, I just got some new crayons. You want to come over and make some pretty Mother's Day cards for our mommies?

Taylor: Yeah! That sounds fun!

Jordan: Okay, let's go!

Taylor and Jordan: Bye! See y'all later!

Questions:

Do you love your mommy?

Does God like for us to listen to our mommies? (Yes.)

Anger

Memory Verses

And "Don't sin by letting anger control you." Don't let the sun go down while you are still angry. Ephesians 4:26

Get rid of all bitterness, rage, anger, harsh words and slander, as well as all types of evil behavior. Ephesians 4:31

Taylor: Ugh!

Jordan: Hey!

Taylor: What?!

Jordan: What's the matter with you?

Taylor: I am so angry!

Jordan: Angry? Why are you angry?

Taylor: I have been trying to learn how to tie my shoes by myself and I can't do it!

Jordan: Well just because you can't do it right now doesn't mean you aren't ever going to learn.

Taylor: Yeah, but I keep trying and trying and I never get better, so I keep getting angry.

Jordan: Well, I can tell you right now, getting angry won't help you any.

Taylor: I know, but sometimes it is really easy to get angry.

Jordan: Yes, you're right, it is easy. But God doesn't like us to be angry.

Taylor: He doesn't?

Jordan: Nope. In fact, anger is talked about a lot in the Bible.

Taylor: Maybe next time I try to tie my shoes I need to just stop and pray that God will give me patience and He will show me what I need to do.

Jordan: You know what, that is a great idea. I remember this one time I was trying to learn how to ride my bike, and every time I started going, I would fall down.

Taylor: Oh, no! I bet you got angry didn't you?

Jordan: At first, yes I did. But then my daddy came out to help me and showed me what I needed to do to get going.

Taylor: Well, that was very nice of him.

Jordan: This one time I was going and then I crashed right into a tree!

Taylor: Oh my goodness, were you okay?

Jordan: Yes, I was fine.

Taylor: Okay, good.

Jordan: But I learned that getting mad and angry didn't help any. I was learning something new and sometimes that can take a little while to do.

Taylor: Yeah.

Jordan: The Bible says in Ephesians 4:26 "Don't sin by letting anger control you. Don't let the sun go down while you are still angry."

Taylor: What does that mean?

Jordan: That just means, don't go do something bad just because you are mad and angry. And don't go to sleep angry either.

Taylor: Oh, I see. That's a good verse.

Jordan: Hey, how about we go try to tie some shoes? I'll help you.

Taylor: Okay, yeah, I think I am ready to try again now.

Jordan: Alright. (to kids) Bye!

Taylor: Bye!

Questions:

Is it good to be angry? (No.)

Should we go do something bad because we're angry? (No.)

Does God like us to be angry or happy? (Happy.)

Friendship

Taylor: Hey. What are you doing?

Jordan: I'm getting this bag of goodies ready for my new neighbor. She's the same age as me, and she likes everything I like. I'm going over to her house right now. She has a big swimming pool with a huge twisty slide!

Taylor: You're not going to start spending more time with her than me, are you?

Jordan: No, never! You're my best friend.

Taylor: So, we are still going to the park today, right?

Jordan: Oh, well, she has tickets to the circus.

Taylor: Oh, that sounds like so much fun! What time are we going?

Jordan: Um, Taylor.

Taylor: What are we going to wear? (goes down and starts throwing clothes in the air.)

Jordan: Taylor. (Dodges clothes.)

Taylor: Should I wear this? Or this?

Jordan: Taylor!

Taylor: Or maybe this?

Jordan: TAYLOR!

Taylor: (comes up) Yeah?

Jordan: She only has two tickets.

Taylor: Oh.

Jordan: Hey, we could go to the park Friday.

Taylor: (Sad) Yeah. Ok, well, sure. Have fun.

Jordan: Ok, thanks. You're such a good friend. (leaves)

Taylor: Man, she won't want to be my friend anymore. I don't have a swimming pool or a big twisty slide. (Leaves.)

TEACHER: Wow. Taylor sure is sad. Why is she so sad? What do you think? Do you think Jordan will still want to be Taylor's friend? Let's watch and see.

Jordan: Hey, I'm back from the circus.

Taylor: (Sad) Oh, did you have fun?

Jordan: Yeah! I got a really cool hat, and a stuffed tiger, and I ate blue cotton candy and it turned my tongue blue!

Taylor: Oh, yeah, that's really cool.

Jordan: Hey, what's wrong? You seem sad.

Taylor: Well, now you're friends with her. You're not friends with me anymore.

Jordan: Of course I am! I still want to be your friend. You can have more than one friend. I'm sorry. I didn't mean to hurt your feelings. Hey, I'll make it up to you. I'll order a pepperoni pizza and you pick out a movie.

Taylor: Okay. Hey, let's invite your new friend over to hang out with us. Like you said. You can have more than one friend.

Jordan: Yeah!

Taylor: Okay, come on let's go!

Jordan: Hey! Wait for me!

Questions:
Was Taylor sad that Jordan had another friend? (Yes.)
We can have more than one friend, can't we? (Yes.)

Giving

Memory Verses

For God so loved the world that He gave His only begotten Son, that whoever believes in Him shall not perish but have everlasting life. John 3:16

Taylor: No mom! I don't want that one! I want the pink one. And I want a pony. But not just a pony. I want a white one. And I want a swimming pool, and a tv, and a guitar, and a swing set with a big slide on it, and a pet monkey! Oh, Jordan is here. I have to go. Bye.

Jordan: What were you doing?

Taylor: Oh, I was just telling my mom what I want for Christmas.

Jordan: Wow! That's a lot of stuff! What would you even do with all that stuff anyways?

Taylor: Play with it.

Jordan: I mean that's just a lot of stuff for one little girl. What are you giving your mom for Christmas?

Taylor: Well I haven't really thought about that. But she's hard to buy for. My daddy will get her something.

Jordan: But don't you want to get her something to show her how much you love her?

Taylor: Oh, she knows I love her. She's my mommy.

Jordan: Well, how would you feel if she didn't get you anything?

Taylor: What? Not get me anything for Christmas?!

Jordan: Yeah. Wouldn't you be sad?

Taylor: I sure would!

Jordan: Well, just think about how she will feel. You asking her for all that stuff and not getting her anything.

Taylor: Well, I didn't thing about that.

Jordan: Christmas is about giving. Not getting. John 3:16 says, "For God so loved the world that He gave His only begotten Son, that whoever believes in Him shall not perish but have everlasting life." God gave His Son as a gift. Because He loves us.

Taylor: He does?

Jordan: He sure does. Christmas is about giving, and celebrating Jesus' birthday, and God's gift of eternal life.

Taylor: Well, I never thought of that before.

Jordan: Yeah, even the wise men brought baby Jesus gifts.

Taylor: I guess maybe I should get her something. And maybe take a few things off my list.

Jordan: Yeah. I mean seriously? A pet monkey?

Taylor: Hey. Don't tell me you wouldn't like to have a pet monkey.

Jordan: Yeah. That would be awesome!

Taylor: I know! So what was that verse again?

Jordan: You mean John 3:16?

Taylor: Yeah. Could you say that again so I can learn it?

Jordan: Sure. Y'all say it with us.

Taylor and Jordan: "For God so loved the world that He gave His only begotten Son, that whoever believes in Him shall not perish but have everlasting life."

Taylor: You want to go shopping with me to find something for my mom?

Jordan: Sure. Maybe we can find her a pet monkey.

Taylor and Jordan leave laughing.

Questions:
Is Christmas about getting lots of gifts? (No.)
Is Christmas about giving? (Yes.)

Heaven

Taylor: Hey!

Jordan: Hey.

Taylor: I came to say goodbye.

Jordan: What? Where are you going?

Taylor: My family is going to the beach!

Jordan: Ooh, that sounds fun.

Taylor: I'm going to build a sand castle and hunt for sea shells, and go swimming. I can't wait to see the beach!

Jordan: Yeah, the beach is beautiful. But I can't wait to see Heaven!

Taylor: What's so great about Heaven?

Jordan: What's so great about Heaven?! EVERYTHING!

Taylor: I thought it was just riding on clouds eating marshmallows and singing all day. I like marshmallows but not that much.

Jordan: What? No! That's not what Heaven is like. Heaven is paradise! The streets are made of gold!

Taylor: Real gold?

Jordan: Yes. And the river is so clear and pretty. Not muddy and dirty. And it's never night time.

Taylor: So I won't need my night light in Heaven?

Jordan: Nope. You will never have to be scared of the dark again because it's so bright and beautiful all the time! And there is no pain in Heaven.

Taylor: No pain at all?

Jordan: Nope. You won't ever have another boo-boo. And Jesus said He will wipe our tears away. You'll never be sad again! And you know the best part?

Taylor: What?

Jordan: Jesus will be there. We will get to spend forever with Him!

Taylor: Forever?

Jordan: Forever and ever!

Taylor: How do you get to Heaven? I want to go!

Jordan: Well, first you have to know you're a sinner.

Taylor: What's that mean?

Jordan: That means we sometimes do bad things. But if we are sorry, God will forgive us. The Bible says that all have sinned. And the punishment for sin is death. But Jesus died for us so we could go to Heaven.

Taylor: He did?

Jordan: Yes. And the Bible says in John 10:9 "If you say out loud that Jesus is Lord and believe in your heart that God raised him from the dead, you will be saved.

Taylor: Jordan? I want to be saved so I can go to Heaven.

Jordan: All you have to do is say this simple prayer. Repeat after me. Dear Jesus, I know I am a sinner.

Taylor: Dear Jesus, I know I am a sinner.

Jordan: I'm sorry for my sins and I ask you to forgive me.

Taylor: I'm sorry for my sins and I ask you to forgive me.

Jordan: I know that Jesus is Lord.

Taylor: I know that Jesus is Lord.

Jordan: And I believe that He died and rose from the dead.

Taylor: And I believe that He died and rose from the dead.

Jordan: Thank you for dying for me so I can go to Heaven.

Taylor: Thank you for dying for me so I can go to Heaven.

Jordan: Please come into my heart and save me.

Taylor: Please come into my heart and save me.

Jordan: And help me to be more like You every day.

Taylor: And help me to be more like You every day.

Jordan: In Jesus name, Amen.

Taylor: In Jesus name, Amen. Thank you so much for teaching me about Heaven and how to be saved!

Jordan: You're very welcome. I'm so happy for you!

Taylor: I'm so excited! I'm going to go tell all my family about it!

Jordan: Ok! Have fun on your trip! See you when you get back!

Questions:
Will we be sad in Heaven? (No.)
Will we be happy in Heaven? (Yes.)
Will Jesus be in Heaven? (Yes.)

Joy

Memory Verses

Come, everyone! Clap your hands! Shout to God with joyful praise! Psalm 47:1

Shout to the Lord, all the earth; break out in praise and sing for joy! Psalm 66:1

Taylor: Joy… joy… joy… down in my HEART!

Jordan: Hey, what are you…

Taylor: Guess what?

Jordan: What?

Taylor: I've got the joy, joy, joy, joy down in my heart!

Jordan: Where?

Taylor: Down in my heart!

Jordan: Where?

Taylor: Down in my heart!

Jordan: Well, that's great to hear!

Taylor: Yeah, and guess why!

Jordan: Umm… because you're…

Taylor: So happy, so very happy! I have the love of Jesus in my heart!

Jordan: Wow, yes you do!

Taylor: (Dancing and being silly while humming.)

Jordan: And you know, that makes God very happy.

Taylor: It does?

Jordan: Yes! In Psalms 66:1 it says "shout for joy to God, all the earth!"

Taylor: Yeah! And if the devil doesn't like it, he can sit on a tack!

Jordan: That is what you are doing. You are singing and shouting for joy for all to hear.

Taylor: Well I am just happy I have such a wonderful God who brings me all this joy every day.

Jordan: And I am happy God gave me a friend like you to remind me that I need to do the same thing.

Taylor: Yeah, well we can all have bad days.

Jordan: But who can have a bad day when you go around singing about joy?

Taylor: You are right about that!

Jordan: When I say "I've got", you say "Joy!" I've got...

Taylor: Joy!

Jordan: I've got...

Taylor: Joy!

Taylor and Jordan: I've got the joy, joy, joy, joy, down in my heart. Where? Down in my heart! Where? Down in my heart! I've got the joy, joy, joy, joy, down in my heart. Down in my heart to stay! And I'm so happy, so very happy. I have the love of Jesus in my heart!

Taylor: I love that song!

Jordan: Me, too!

Taylor: I've got so much joy I want to tell the whole world about it!

Jordan: Well, let's go!

Taylor: Right now?

Jordan: Why not?

Taylor: Ok! See y'all later!

Jordan: Bye!

Questions:
Do you have joy?
Does God like for us to have joy? (Yes.)

Lying

Taylor: Hey!

Jordan: Hey!

Taylor: How are you today, friend?

Jordan: I am very excited!

Taylor: Why is that?

Jordan: Well, I love getting to see all of our friends. And look how many came to see us today.

Taylor: I know! Hey, we should tell them a story.

Jordan: Okay! A story about what?

Taylor: How about we talk about lying?

Jordan: Wait, what is lying again?

Taylor: You know, when you tell someone something that isn't really true.

Jordan: Oh, I remember a time I got in trouble for lying to my mom.

Taylor: Uh oh. What did you lie about?

Jordan: Well, I wanted to go over to my friend's house to stay the night…

Taylor: Uh huh.

Jordan: And my mom said I could go if I picked up all my toys.

Taylor: So you picked them up, didn't you?

Jordan: Actually… I told her I did, but I didn't.

Taylor: What did you do with them?

Jordan: I took all my toys and shoved them in my closet so she wouldn't see them.

Taylor: Why did you do that?

Jordan: Well, I thought she wouldn't notice… but um… she did. And I got in trouble.

Taylor: Uh oh.

Jordan: She came in and opened my closet and all the toys fell on top of her! Then she stepped on a toy car and slipped and her feet went way up in the air! Luckily she landed on my stuffed teddy bear.

Taylor: Wow. That sure wasn't very nice to lie to your mommy. She could have gotten hurt.

Jordan: I know. I felt really bad after I did it.

Taylor: What did you learn from it?

Jordan: Well, I learned that lying to my mommy isn't a way to show her I love her.

Taylor: That's right!

Jordan: Yeah, if I really want to show how much I love her, I need to clean up all my toys and put them where they go.

Taylor: That is exactly right.

Jordan: Have you ever lied before?

Taylor: Well, I am not proud of it, but yes I have.

Jordan: Really?

Taylor: Yes. And lying is a sin. Sometimes lying can even hurt other people.

Jordan: I told my mommy I was sorry after I lied.

Taylor: That's great! We also need to say we're sorry to God when we lie.

Jordan: He doesn't like for us to lie.

Taylor: No, He doesn't.

Jordan: But if we have Him in our heart, we can ask Him to forgive us for that.

Taylor: That's just another awesome thing about God.

Jordan: He loves us so much.

Taylor: Well, thanks for sharing your story and the lesson that you learned with us.

Jordan: You're welcome. (To kids) Thank you for coming and listening.

Taylor: See you later!

Taylor and Jordan: Bye!

Questions:

Does God like for us to lie? (No.)

Is lying a way to show we love someone? (No.)

Patience & Self-Control

Taylor: Hey!

Jordan: Hey.

Taylor: How are you?

Jordan: My tummy hurts.

Taylor: Oh no, are you sick?

Jordan: Kind of.

Taylor: What do you have?

Jordan: Well, you see… my mommy was going to make some cookies and… um… I…

Taylor: What did you do?

Jordan: Well, I really, really wanted some and I didn't want to wait for her to make them.

Taylor: Uh, huh.

Jordan: So… when she left to go to the bathroom, I grabbed the cookie dough, went to my room and ate the whole bowl!

Taylor: THE WHOLE BOWL?!

Jordan: Yes! (starts crying)

Taylor: Oh my, I bet you do have a tummy ache.

Jordan: I do, and my mommy was not very happy with me either.

Taylor: What did she say?

Jordan: She said next time I need to be more patient and have self-control. Whatever that means.

Taylor: That means just because you think you wanted to eat all that cookie dough, you should have waited until they were cooked and only ate a couple of them.

Jordan: Oh. But they just looked sooooo yummy and I thought I couldn't wait any longer.

Taylor: I know. Sometimes it's hard to have patience.

Jordan: Does God like for us to have patience?

Taylor: He sure does. He even talks about it in the Bible.

Jordan: Really?

Taylor: Yes. In Proverbs 16:32 it says, "Better to be patient than (strong, mighty, great); better to have self-control than to crush a city.

Jordan: You know what?

Taylor: What?

Jordan: I am going to pray that God will give me patience and self-control.

Taylor: That is a great idea!

Jordan: I don't ever want to have a tummy ache like this again.

Taylor: Well, I don't want you to either.

Jordan: I think I am going to go take some medicine and tell my mommy that next time I will help her make the cookies, not eat all of them before she can cook them.

Taylor: Okay, well I'll see you later!

Taylor and Jordan: Bye!

Questions:

Does God want us to have patience and self-control? (Yes.)

Will you get a tummy ache if you eat a whole bowl of cookie dough? (Yes.)

Prayer

Taylor: Hey!

Jordan: Hi. (sad.)

Taylor: What's the matter?

Jordan: God's not answering my prayers!

Taylor: What do you mean?

Jordan: Well I really, really, want a puppy. So I asked God if He would give me one. But I keep praying and I still don't have a puppy!

Taylor: Well, that doesn't mean God isn't answering your prayers.

Jordan: Then where is my puppy?

Taylor: Okay, I have a question?

Jordan: Okay.

Taylor: Can I have your bike?

Jordan: What? Why do you need that?

Taylor: Exactly! I don't need it.

Jordan: Then why did you ask me for it?

Taylor: I'm trying to show you, that sometimes we ask God for things we don't really need. We just want them.

Jordan: Oh… So maybe God isn't really not answering my prayers. He is just saying maybe I don't need a puppy right now.

Taylor: That's right. I mean, it is very important for us to pray. And it is okay to ask for things.

Jordan: Right. And if it is what God thinks we need, He will give it to us.

Taylor: That's right!

Jordan: Well, I really do want a puppy, but I know when God thinks I am ready to have one He will give me one.

Taylor: Yes He will.

Jordan: Wow, thank you so much for teaching me that.

Taylor: You are welcome! Now is there anything else you really need that we can pray about?

Jordan: Yes. My little sister is sick and I really need her to get better so she can play with me again.

Taylor: Okay, let's pray. Jesus, thank you for taking care of us while we are sick, and making us feel better. Just like I know you will do for Jordan's little sister. Amen.

Jordan: Thank you!

Taylor: You're welcome. Well, I gotta go. I'll see you later!

Jordan: Okay. Bye!

Questions:

Is it important for us to pray? (Yes.)

Does He always give us what we want? (No.)

But He always gives us what we need doesn't He? (Yes.)

Sharing

Memory Verses

Cheerfully share your home with those who need a meal or a place to stay. 1 Peter 4:9

And don't forget to do good and to share with those in need. These are the things that please God. Hebrews 13:16

Taylor: Hey guys!

Jordan: Guess what I got for my birthday!

Taylor: What?

Jordan: I got a bike!

Taylor: No way! Really?

Jordan: Yeah! It's so much fun! But it's so annoying. My little sister always wants to ride it, too. It's my bike. I'm not letting her ride it.

Taylor: Well, it is yours. But don't you think you could share a little bit?

Jordan: What? I don't want to share with my little sister? No way! It's my bike! Why should I share?

Taylor: Well, the Bible tells us to share. It says in 1 Timothy 6:18 that we should always be ready to share with others.

Jordan: Well, yeah, but it's my bike. She might scratch it.

Taylor: "And don't forget to do good and to share with those in need. These are the things that please God." Hebrews 13:16

Jordan: But what if she runs into something and crashes it.

Taylor: "And God will generously provide all you need. Then you will always have everything you need and plenty left over to share with others." 2 Corinthians 9:8

Jordan: Well, yeah, but…

Taylor: I got more. "Cheerfully share your home with those who need a meal or a place to stay." 1 Peter 4:9

Jordan: Ok, ok! I guess I should share with others.

Taylor: Come on. Sharing isn't so bad. Think about how it pleases God when we share. And how happy it makes other people. And God also blesses those who share.

Jordan: Well, I guess God has given me with everything I need. And now He is giving me things I want. Like a bike. So I guess I could share with others.

Taylor: That's right.

Jordan: You wanna come over and ride bikes with me?

Taylor: I would love to!

Jordan: And I guess my sister can ride with us.

Taylor: Well that's very nice of you.

Questions:

Do any of you have brothers or sisters?

Do you share your toys with them?

Do they share things with you?

Does sharing make God happy? (Yes.)

AWANA Night

Jordan: Well, here we are. It's Wednesday. Again.

Taylor: What? You sound so sad. Today is church day! AWANA day!

Jordan: Church day, AWANA day. What's so great about that?

Taylor: We get to wear cool shirts and learn Bible verses!

Jordan: I would rather stay home and watch cartoons. Now that's fun!

Taylor: Yeah. But when you're lonely or sad, how do cartoons help you?

Jordan: What do you mean?

Taylor: When I'm sad or lonely I can remember Bible verses, or I can pray and spend time with Jesus. Then I feel much better!

Jordan: I just eat a big yummy bowl of ice cream! But then I usually get a stomach ache after.

Taylor: Spending time at church won't give you a stomach ache. Jesus wants to spend time with you.

Jordan: Why does Jesus want to spend time with me?

Taylor: Because He loves you. And He thinks you're great!

Jordan: He does?

Taylor: Yep. He wants to get to know you better.

Jordan: How do I get to know Him better?

Taylor: When you sing, pray, and read your Bible, that helps you get to know Him. And when you go to church, you get to meet other people who love Jesus.

Jordan: Yeah, but I saw some kids from church hitting another kid. They weren't acting like Jesus.

Taylor: Yeah, but when we go to church, we are supposed to focus on God. Not what the other kids are doing.

Jordan: But I like knowing what other kids do in church. I want to watch them and do what they do, and be just like them.

Taylor: Well, you can pray about that. It's better to try and be like Jesus.

Jordan: Can we pray that Jesus will help me to go to church, and get to know Him better, and be more like Him?

Taylor: Sure! Let's bow our heads and pray right now.

Jordan: Okay.

Taylor: Dear Jesus, please help my friend get to know You better. And help us to be more like You. Amen.

Jordan: Thank you. You know what? I do feel better. I think I will go to church tonight.

Taylor: Awesome! You'll get a book, and a bag. And you'll get a vest or a shirt. And we will get to learn Bible verses!

Jordan: Cool!

Taylor: Don't forget to bring your Bible!

Jordan: Okay. See you tonight!

Questions:
Do you go to AWANAs?
AWANAs is really fun. Find a friend this week and invite them to AWANAs.

Printed in the United States
By Bookmasters